HISTORY IN LITERATURE
THE STORY BEHIND...

GEORGE ORWELL'S
ANIMAL FARM

Alan Brown

Heinemann
LIBRARY

www.heinemann.co.uk/library

Visit our website to find out more information about Heinemann Library books.

To order:

☎ Phone 44 (0) 1865 888066

🖹 Send a fax to 44 (0) 1865 314091

💻 Visit the Heinemann Bookshop at www.heinemann.co.uk/library to browse our catalogue and order online.

First published in Great Britain by
Heinemann Library, Halley Court, Jordan Hill,
Oxford, OX2 8EJ, part of Harcourt Education.
Heinemann is a registered trademark of
Harcourt Education Ltd.

© Harcourt Education Ltd 2007
The moral right of the proprietor has

Editorial: Louise Galpine, Lucy Beevor,
  and Rosie Gordon
Design: Richard Parker and
  Manhattan Design
Picture Research: Melissa Allison and
  Elaine Willis
Production: Chloe Bloom

Originated by Modern Age
Printed and bound in China by Leo Paper Group

10 digit ISBN 0 431 08168 9
13 digit ISBN 978 0 431 08168 7

11 10 09 08 07
10 9 8 7 6 5 4 3 2 1

British Library Cataloguing in Publication Data
Brown, Alan
The story behind George Orwell's *Animal Farm*.
– (History in literature)
823.9'12
A full catalogue record for this book is
available from the British Library.

Acknowledgements
The publishers would like to thank the following
for permission to reproduce photographs/quotes:
akg-images p. 21; Bridgeman Art Library pp. 33,
36 (Halas & Batchelor Collection Ltd.); Corbis
p. 8; Corbis pp. 14, 26, 34, 38, 43, 46, 47
(Bettmann), 28 (Hulton-Deutsch Collection),
25 (The Dmitri Baltermants Collection), 16
(Sygma/Pierre Vauthey), 17 (Yevgeny Khaldei);
Empics p. 42 (AP); George Orwell Archives,
University College London p.24; Getty Images pp.
12 (Hulton Archive/Picture Post), 22 (Keystone),
35 (Time Life Pictures), 39 (Time Life Pictures/
Alfred Eisenstaedt), 4 (Time Life Pictures/Chris
Niedenthal), 37 (Time Life Pictures/ Pix Inc.);
Illustrated London News p.11; Mary
Evans Picture Library pp. 9, 31, p. 29 (Weimar
Archive); Popperfoto p. 15; TopFoto.co.uk p. 19,
p. 44 (PAL); UCL Library Services, Special
Collections, Orwell Archives pp. 5, 6, 10, 13,
18, 20, 23, 27, 30, 32, 40, 41, 45, 48, 49.

1) Animal Farm by George Orwell © George
Orwell 1945 by permission of Bill Hamilton as
the Literary Executor of the Estate of the Late
Sonia Brownell Orwell and Secker & Warburg Ltd
3)) p29 – Reproduced with permission of
Curtis Brown on behalf of The Estate of Winston
Churchill.

Cover photograph of George Orwell and
photographs in background reproduced with
permission of Getty Images/Hulton Archive.

The publishers would like to thank Professor
Peter Davison for his assistance in the
preparation of this book.

Every effort has been made to contact copyright
holders of any material reproduced in this book.
Any omissions will be rectified in subsequent
printings if notice is given to the publishers.

Contents

Some words are shown in bold, **like this**. You can find out what they mean by looking in the glossary.

If pigs could fly

Animal Farm is one of the most important political stories ever written. From the time of its publication in 1945, it has been a constant best-seller, which has been translated into more than seventy languages and read by millions. It is a short book – less than a hundred pages long – telling the story of how animals overthrow their human masters in an attempt to set up a fairer society. Behind this simple farmyard tale is a fierce **analysis** of the abuse of political power, and of how our hopes for a better future can be destroyed.

George Orwell wrote *Animal Farm* to show how the ideas of the **Russian Revolution** were betrayed by its leaders. Early in the story, the animals paint a series of slogans, or "commandments", on to the barn wall. The most important of these is: "All animals are equal." Later in the novel the power-hungry leaders turn the slogan on its head by adding "But some animals are more equal than others."

ALL ANIMALS ARE EQUAL
~
BUT SOME ANIMALS ARE MORE EQUAL THAN OTHERS.

This is a bust of Joseph Stalin, who ruled over the former Soviet Union from the 1920s until his death in 1953. His harsh **dictatorship** is the target of *Animal Farm*, one of the last novels written by George Orwell.

Prose like a window pane

Orwell had an ability to express complex ideas in simple and memorable language. He spent many years working on his style, throwing away whole manuscripts because he was not happy with them. He believed that good writing should reveal the world as clearly as possible, and that "Good **prose** is like a window pane".

Animal Farm was written at the height of World War II, when the Russians were fighting alongside the **Allies** against Hitler's **Nazi** regime. Many people thought it was wrong to criticize a nation that was on "our side", but Orwell refused to accept public opinion. He was always looking for a different viewpoint – even in a time of war. He wanted to provoke an argument and he was not going to keep silent. We are still arguing about his work today.

George Orwell broadcasting for the British Broadcasting Corporation (BBC) during World War II. Orwell believed that the BBC was "very truthful" but he hated "the unbearable voices of its announcers".

Orwell and his wife Sonia experienced the daily bombing of London at first hand during World War II. In the essay "England Your England" (1941), he wrote:

> *As I write, highly civilized human beings are flying overhead, trying to kill me. They are only 'doing their duty' as the saying goes. Most of them, I have no doubt, are kind-hearted law-abiding men who would never dream of committing murder in private life. On the other hand, if one of them succeeds in blowing me to pieces with a well-placed bomb, he will never sleep any the worse for it.*

Introducing Eric Blair

George Orwell is widely known as a writer of political novels and essays. It is less well known that he was born with another name and chose "George Orwell" as his **pen name** when his first book was published.

Orwell was born Eric Arthur Blair in Bengal, India, in 1903. At that time India was part of the **British Empire** and a military government ruled its people. Eric was the second child of Richard Blair and Ida Limouzin who married in India in 1896.

Eric was five months old when his mother brought him back to England. The family settled near London and his father returned to work in colonial India. Eric had only vague childhood memories of his father. He later recalled him as, "A gruff-voiced elderly man forever saying 'Don't'."

THE BRITISH EMPIRE

At the beginning of the 1900s, Great Britain was the world's largest power, ruling some 500 million people around the globe. European nations, beginning with Spain and Portugal, had been exploring the world and invading new territories since the 1400s. They seized the wealth of the countries they **colonized***, and ruled their populations. At the time of Orwell's birth, the British Empire contained around a quarter of the world's population and territory – some 15 million square miles (39 million square kilometres).*

Eric Blair as a five-month-old baby, cradled by his Indian nanny. His mother took him back to England at the end of 1903.

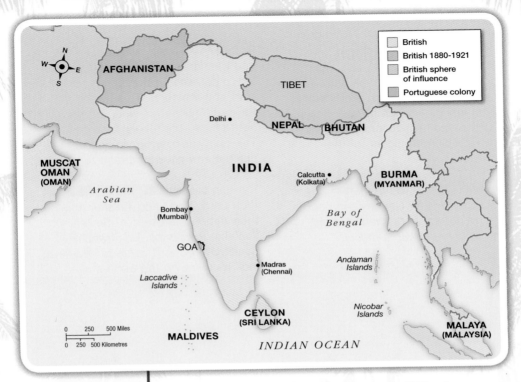

A map showing the Indian sub-continent in 1921, when Eric Blair returned to the region at the age of nineteen. Place names are labelled as Blair would have known them during colonial times, with current names shown in parentheses.

When he was eight years old Eric was sent to a boarding school, St Cyprian's, where he studied hard and was deeply unhappy. In 1916, he won a scholarship to England's most famous **public school**, Eton. This should have led him to a successful and comfortable future. But he surprised everyone five years later when he decided not to go on to university. At the age of nineteen, Eric Blair followed in his father's footsteps and headed for Asia where he joined the military police.

Orwell said of his childhood:

I was the middle child of three, but there was a gap of five years on either side [...] I was somewhat lonely, and I soon developed disagreeable mannerisms which made me unpopular throughout my schooldays. I had the lonely child's habit of making up stories and holding conversations with imaginary persons.

7

A time of revolution

Eric Blair's childhood took place in the shadow of major events. **World War I** began in 1914, when he was eleven. Eric pleased his schoolteachers by writing a **patriotic** poem for the occasion:

"Awake! Oh you young men of England,
For if, when your Country's in need
You do not enlist by the thousand,
You truly are cowards indeed."

In 1917 in Russia, widespread poverty and the harsh rule of **Tsar** Nicholas II led to protests on the streets and the start of a rebellion. This turned into a full-scale revolution when troops, sent out to crush the rebels, changed sides. The Tsar was overthrown and in his place a new government seized control.

Russian **communists**, led by Vladimir Ilich Lenin and Leon Trotsky, renamed their nation the Union of Soviet **Socialist** Republics (USSR). The Soviet Union, as it came to be known, took its place on the world stage.

A group of Russians gather in the snow holding flags during burial ceremonies for victims of the Russian Revolution, March 23, 1917.

The emergence of a powerful nation committed to communist principles, which it was determined to spread worldwide, threatened the ruling powers in Europe and the United States. They were concerned that communist ideas about equality and social justice could spread like a virus and create unrest amongst the poorer classes in the **capitalist** countries. This fierce struggle between **ideologies** – communism and capitalism – became one of the major conflicts of the century.

Karl Marx (1818–1883), the German radical political thinker (date of photograph unknown).

THE IDEAS OF COMMUNISM

*At the time of the Russian Revolution, communists believed that the wealth of a nation – its land, factories, property, and money – should all be used for the **collective** benefit of the people. Communists argued that equality for all citizens would lead to the "withering away" of government. They thought that if there was no struggle between competing interests, there would be no need for a ruling class to control society.*

*Karl Marx, the 19th-century **philosopher** of communism, believed that events in history have a pattern. He argued that all societies will develop through time towards their final goal of a classless and equal society.*

*Under the rule of Joseph Stalin, however, the Soviet Union broke with the original ideas of the revolution. Government became all-powerful and the population was controlled through violence, **surveillance**, and a constant pressure to **conform**. Socialists such as Orwell shared many of the values behind Soviet communism, but totally rejected the anti-democratic and **authoritarian** nature it took on under Stalin.*

Policing the Empire

When Eric Blair left Eton in 1921, aged eighteen, he stepped away from a world of **privilege**. He had always felt like an outsider. He was painfully aware as a child that his parents were not rich and that he did not really "belong" with the **elite**.

In setting sail for Asia to begin his career as a military policeman he was returning to his birthplace. He was also following in his father's footsteps.

Richard Blair had worked as a civil servant for the British Empire supervising the cultivation of crops for the Indian Opium Department.

It was in Burma (now Myanmar) that Eric began to see for himself the huge differences between rich and poor, power and **destitution**. He wrote about his experiences, and began to fulfill his childhood dream of becoming "Eric the Great Writer".

Eric (third from the left in the back row) at the Police Training School in Mandalay, Burma.

OPIUM AND THE EMPIRE

Opium was first used in China in the 15th century as a medicine. The drug was also smoked for pleasure and created large numbers of addicts. In the 18th century, Britain began to sell Indian-grown opium to Chinese merchants in exchange for tea. Attempts by China to stop the flow of British opium led to two wars in which China was defeated. Britain finally agreed to end their opium trade in 1917.

Eric Blair spent six years working for the military police in Burma. From the start, he was unhappy with his status as a member of the ruling elite. On Blair's journey to Rangoon (Burma's capital city) in 1922, during a stopover in Colombo, Ceylon (Sri Lanka), Blair looked on as a white policeman on the dock kicked a local **coolie**. He was shocked by what he saw, and by the responses of his fellow passengers:

"Here were ordinary, decent, middling people [. . .] watching the scene with no emotion whatever except a mild approval. They were white, and the coolie was black. In other words he was sub-human, a different kind of animal."

Blair was put in charge of around 200 local men, policing a population of 200,000 in the region of Hanthawaddy. It was a heavy responsibility for a young man of 21, especially because he felt sympathy towards the very people he was meant to keep under control.

THE WHIP HAND

After a lifetime of being beaten and abused, like the coolie in Rangoon, the animals turn on their masters in Chapter Two of *Animal Farm:*

Jones and his men suddenly found themselves being butted and kicked from all sides. The situation was quite out of their control. They had never seen anything like this before, and this sudden uprising of creatures whom they were used to thrashing and maltreating just as they chose, frightened them almost out of their wits.

Eric's account of his experiences in Asia was published as a novel called *Burmese Days* in 1934. It included a stinging attack on the British Empire. Many of the Burmese-British were offended by the novel. Cline Stewart, the head of the police training school, said that if he ever saw Blair again he would "horsewhip him".

Sir Charles Innes, who was made Governor of Burma in 1927, thanks Burmese village headmen for their services on completion of his term as Governor. His authority over the Burmese is clear in this photograph.

Down and out

Eric Blair returned to England in 1927 and resigned his job with the Imperial Police on January 1, 1928. "I gave it up," he explained, "partly because the climate ruined my health, partly because I had vague ideas of writing a book, but mostly because I could not go on any longer serving an **imperialism** that I had come to regard as very largely a **racket**."

The England he came back to was in serious crisis. Workers who had fought for their country in World War I now faced huge wage cuts or, worse, no jobs at all. A year earlier, in 1926, British workers, led by the miners, held a **strike** that temporarily brought the nation to a standstill. They gained little, however, and the gap between rich and poor continued to widen.

England was a divided nation and arguments over the possible ways forward – socialism, capitalism, communism, or **fascism** – filled the newspapers and magazines.

Working-class families lived in cramped and filthy conditions in city slums in the United Kingdom, such as the family seen here in Glasgow, Scotland.

Orwell explained his early thinking about poverty and politics in *The Road to Wigan Pier*, published in 1937:

I had reduced everything to the simple theory that the oppressed are always right and the oppressors are always wrong: a mistaken theory, but the natural result of being one of the oppressors yourself. I wanted to submerge myself, to get right down among the oppressed, to be one of them and on their side against the tyrants.

Eric moved to London to make his way as a writer. He worked part-time in a bookshop and spent hours in a rented attic, tapping away at an old typewriter – warming his hands over a candle before starting. He was determined to master his new trade.

At the same time Eric began to go on **tramping** expeditions, joining the **underclass** of unemployed men and women who slept rough and walked the streets. On one occasion he got himself arrested so that he could see the inside of a jail at first hand. From these experiences he later wrote his first published book, *Down and Out in Paris and London*.

Eric Blair dressing down for his tramping expeditions in the late 1920s. His friend Brenda Salkend argued that he could not really know what it was like to be a tramp "because he could always get away back home".

In 1929 he moved to Paris where he wrote articles (five of which were published in French), short stories, and a couple of novels (none of which were published). Eric became destitute, and for about three months he worked as a dishwasher in a grimy restaurant kitchen. He slept in shabby, unheated rooms and eventually ended up in the charity ward of a hospital after a severe attack of **bronchitis**. He later wrote about this experience in a horrifying essay called "How the Poor Die". At this time, Eric Blair seemed driven towards **squalor** and suffering, and eventually he would pay for it with the breakdown of his health.

WRITING AND TRAMPING

There is a long history of writers as tramps in UK and US literature. Mark Twain's autobiographical stories offer humorous accounts of the tramp as a "free spirit". Jack London wrote The People of the Abyss after living amongst the poorest communities in London and studying their poverty at first hand. W. H. Davies, who published his Autobiography of a Super-Tramp in 1908, later wrote a favourable review of Orwell's work.

The age of extremes

As the 1920s ended, Europe and the United States were in economic trouble. The **Wall Street Crash** of 1929 marked the beginning of the "Great Depression" in the United States. In the United Kingdom, mass unemployment led to outbreaks of violence as supporters of opposing political systems fought for control of the streets.

Germany suffered extreme upheavals after its defeat in World War I. Mass poverty and a sense of national humiliation at losing the war led to the formation of new political movements. The most important of these were the fascists led by Adolf Hitler. Hitler's Nazi Party took power in 1933, only fourteen years after its founding. The Nazis wanted to restore national pride and get rid of what they called the *Untermensch* (Subhuman) elements of German society; mainly the Jews, gypsies, homosexuals, and the disabled.

Ranks of German troops enter the Sudetenland in Czechoslovakia, 1939. The British and French leaders handed over the territory to Hitler in September 1938 in a last-ditch attempt to avert a war.

WHAT IS FASCISM?

Fascism is a system of dictatorship with the idea of the "nation" at its centre. Individual freedom is sacrificed to the leader's will, and racial or ethnic purity is harshly enforced. Fascist countries exist in a constant state of war – against enemies inside and outside their borders. The word "fascism" was first used to describe the rule of Benito Mussolini. He seized power in Italy in 1922. Fascism came to be widely associated with Hitler's beliefs and the rise of the Nazis in the 1930s.

Lost paradise

Many of the people who were against fascism in Europe and the United States were communists. They believed that Hitler's Nazis were driven by hatred and military aggression. They looked, instead, to the Soviet Union for a model of social harmony and working for the good of all.

After Lenin, the first Soviet leader, died in 1924, there were signs that communism was being replaced by a brutal **regime**. The new Soviet leader was Joseph Stalin. Reports started to come out suggesting that Stalin's political opponents were being executed and free speech had been stamped out. Russian farmers and land workers were also being driven from their land or executed to make way for new agricultural and industrial projects.

Not everyone believed these claims. Many on the **Left** dismissed the reports as **propaganda**. They were convinced that enemies of communism – in governments and the media – were trying to destroy hope, and preserve the current political systems. But the evidence of Stalin's crimes continued to grow.

THE RISE OF STALIN

*Joseph Stalin was a key figure in the founding of the Soviet Union. He played an important political role during the civil war from 1918 to 1920. This was fought between the "Reds" (communists) and the "Whites" (non-communists who opposed the **Bolshevik** Revolution of 1917). Another senior communist, Leon Trotsky, was in charge of military strategy. After Lenin's death in 1924, Stalin organized support against Trotsky and moved himself into a position of total power. He kept control by creating a world of **paranoia** among Communist Party officials and the population in general. In Stalin's world, no one was safe and no one could be trusted.*

From left to right: Joseph Stalin, Vladimir Lenin, and Leon Trotsky. At first united in the communist cause, Stalin and Trotsky would later feud over the right to Lenin's leadership upon his death.

The great dictator

Animal Farm mirrors the decline of the Soviet Union from its beginnings as a **utopian** project into a period of dictatorship that came to be known as **Stalinism**.

Each phase of the novel suggests a parallel in Soviet history. The farmyard rebellion represents the overthrow of the Russian **monarchy** in 1917. The two pigs, Napoleon and Snowball, represent Joseph Stalin and Leon Trotsky. Their power struggle in the mid-1920s set the course for the future of the Soviet Union.

Napoleon emerges from a "behind-the-scenes" role in the early stages of the story to become the unchallenged ruler of the farm. He is known as "Our Leader" and is celebrated in songs, portraits, and slogans. Napoleon's rise to power parallels the descent into Stalinism, the great betrayal, in George Orwell's view.

Napoleon is incapable of inspiring the other animals with ideas of his own. His strength is in controlling others, in **manipulating** events, and using fear as a weapon. He uses the pig Squealer to persuade the animals, and a pack of dogs to police them. He steals Snowball's ideas for the modernization of the farm and then tries to put them into practice with disastrous results.

Soviet leader Joseph Stalin at the microphone. Stalin himself encouraged the "**cult** of leadership" which grew up during his rule.

The Five Year Plans

In 1928, Stalin announced the first of his Five Year Plans. He hoped to modernize Soviet industry by equipping factories with the latest machinery, generating electricity, and improving transport across the nation. This ambitious scheme was presented to the people as if it promised a new heaven on earth. The plans were poorly thought out and ended largely in chaos. They drained the Soviet economy and this led to widespread hardship. Stalin's response to this failure was to announce yet another Five Year Plan.

A Soviet steelworker at Donetsk Steel Plant, 1934. Soviet artists under Stalin had to produce heroic images of workers building a modern industrial paradise.

The building of the windmill in *Animal Farm* represents the period of the Five Year Plans. Napoleon steals the basic ideas from Snowball, but does not really understand the science and technology and cannot carry them out effectively. Napoleon's power is so strong that no one will question his orders. When the windmill collapses in a storm because the walls are too thin, Napoleon blames Snowball.

To direct attention away from his own mistakes, Napoleon comes up with a plan to blame Snowball instead:

> *'Comrades,' he said quietly, 'do you know who is responsible for this? Do you know the enemy who has come in the night and overthrown our windmill? SNOWBALL!' he suddenly roared in a voice of thunder, 'Snowball has done this thing!'*

Becoming Orwell

Eric Blair's experiences amongst the unemployed in Britain turned him into a socialist and gave him, for the first time, a clear sense of direction as a writer.

In 1932, Eric was contacted by the **left-wing** publisher Victor Gollancz who wanted to publish his account of life amongst the underclass in Paris and London. He was offered £40 (US$70) as an advance on the book. This seems like a small sum of money by today's standards, but the important thing was that his work would appear as a book for the first time. Over the next three years he continued to write, to make very small amounts of money, and to build up his reputation as a writer of both novels and essays.

BLAIR INTO ORWELL

Down and Out in Paris and London was published in 1933 under Eric Blair's pen name, George Orwell. Orwell is the name of a river in the UK countryside, and George is considered the most English of all names (St George is the patron saint of England). The new name protected Eric's family from embarrassment when their son's account of life among the underclass was published.

Eileen O'Shaughnessy married Orwell in 1936. She worked closely with her husband on the early versions of *Animal Farm*.

Two events in 1936 changed George Orwell's life dramatically. In June that year he married Eileen O'Shaughnessy, a psychology student at London University. She shared his political views and supported his writing ambitions.

In the same year his publisher, Gollancz, asked Orwell to travel to the north of England where conditions were hardest, and to write an account of working-class life during the Depression. Orwell lived amongst the unemployed in northern towns and cities, recording details of the lives around him and the grim conditions in which people were forced to live. Out of these experiences, he wrote *The Road to Wigan Pier*.

The Spanish tragedy

Hundreds of miles away in southern Europe, events were unfolding that were also to change Orwell's life. In 1931, popular left-wing protests in Spain led to the peaceful overthrow of the Spanish monarchy, and a **republic** was set up.

Western governments were suspicious of this new regime. Many of Spain's new leading politicians were pro-Soviet and there were fears that communism would spread in Europe. In 1936, the fascist General Francisco Franco led a military revolt against the republic, and this triggered a civil war across Spain.

With the outbreak of the Spanish Civil War, Western governments, including Britain, gave quiet backing to Franco's fascists. They saw him as an **ally** in the battle against communism.

Guernica, Spain, in ruins after the German bombing of 1937.

TERROR FROM THE SKIES

General Franco's greatest ally was Hitler's Germany. The Nazis armed the Spanish fascists. In 1937, German planes were used in the first-ever aerial bombardment in history in which civilians were deliberately chosen as targets. This was in Guernica in northern Spain. Guernica was a testing ground for the Nazis' new philosophy of Die Totale Krieg (Total War). At Guernica, 1,600 people were killed in the bombing and this new threat of destruction from the skies became a widespread fear across Europe.

Fighting the fascists

Orwell went to Spain at the end of 1936, planning to report as a journalist on what he saw. But he quickly picked up on the revolutionary enthusiasm that had swept through Spain and decided to fight on the Republican side.

Many different groups on the Left were fighting against Franco, and Orwell signed up with the first group he was introduced to. It was an organization called POUM (*Partido Obrero de Unificación Marxista*, or "Workers' Party of Marxist Unification").

Orwell was completely unaware of the violent rivalry between left-wing forces in Spain. This was at least as bitter as their shared hostility towards Franco and the fascists. At the heart of this rivalry was the attempt by pro-Stalin communists to control the Republican forces and to stamp out all opposition to the Stalinist line.

Orwell in military training, 1937. He is the tall figure standing directly behind the machine gun. His wife Eileen is sitting close to him.

REVOLUTION ON THE STREETS

In his account of the Spanish Civil War, *Homage to Catalonia*, Orwell described his arrival in Barcelona, Spain, on 26 December 1936:

Practically every building of any size had been seized by the workers. [...] The revolutionary posters were everywhere [...] crowds of people streamed constantly to and fro, the loudspeakers were bellowing revolutionary songs all day [...] Practically everyone wore rough working-class clothes, or blue overalls [...] There was much in it that I did not understand, in some ways I did not even like it, but I recognised it immediately as a state of affairs worth fighting for.

AREN'T WE ALL SOCIALISTS?

Orwell described his confusing arrival at the front-line in Homage to Catalonia:

"At Monte Pocero, when they pointed to the position on our left and said: 'Those are the Socialists' (meaning the PSUC), I was puzzled and said: 'Aren't we all Socialists?' I thought it idiotic that people fighting for their lives should have separate parties; my attitude always was, 'Why can't we drop all this political nonsense and get on with the war?' "

Orwell continued to fight at the front with his comrades through the winter and spring of 1937. He stood alongside them in mud-filled trenches infested with rats and clogged with human waste. It was an ugly, chaotic war, fought with poor equipment and very little strategy. Orwell's fellow soldier and friend, George Kopp, called it "a comic opera with an occasional death".

¡NO PASARÁN!
JULIO 1936

JULIO 1937
¡PASAREMOS!

On leave in Barcelona in May, Orwell was caught up in a full-scale battle across the city between the communists and other anti-fascist groups, including his own POUM militia. He took up a rifle to defend his comrades. Five hundred people died in this gunfight between allies. Orwell's innocent belief that he was fighting a straightforward war against fascism could not survive this latest lesson.

The caption on the poster reads *No Pasaran* (They shall not pass). The blue figure in the helmet is part of General Franco's army. The figure behind is a volunteer for Spain's Republican forces.

General Franco's Nationalist troops enter Barcelona at the end of the Spanish Civil War, 1939.

CLOSE TO DEATH

In his account of the Spanish Civil War, Orwell describes the moment when he was shot by a sniper:

There seemed to be a loud bang and a blinding flash of light all round me, and I felt a tremendous shock – no pain, only a violent shock, such as you get from an electric terminal [...]

Reign of terror

Orwell lived through the bloodbath in Barcelona but he was powerfully affected by what he saw: "It was as though some huge evil intelligence were brooding over the town", he later wrote. "A peculiar evil feeling in the air – an atmosphere of suspicion, uncertainty, and veiled hatred."

He returned to the front to take up arms against the fascists again, but on the morning of 20 May he was shot in the throat while on sentry duty. He was rushed to hospital and, at first, was expected to die. Orwell made a good recovery, although his voice was permanently affected. When he left hospital two weeks later and met his wife Eileen at the Hotel Continental in Barcelona, she hugged him and whispered in his ear: "Get out!".

After the battle between left-wing Republican militias weeks earlier, pro-Stalin forces had begun a full-scale **purge** of their rivals. Using a network of spies and informers, they had drawn up a list of enemies and were now hunting them down. Orwell was on the list. "This was not a round-up of criminals", he later wrote. "It was a reign of terror."

The Orwells escaped across the border into France, but others were not so lucky. Orwell's friend George Kopp was imprisoned for more than a year. Another POUM fighter, Bob Smillie, was thrown into jail where he died soon after. The story was put out that he had died of **appendicitis** – probably because it had been left untreated by his jailers.

Orwell left Spain with a grim new awareness of politics on the Left. He no longer saw any moral difference between the threats posed by fascism and Stalinism. He believed both were distinguished by contempt for the truth and contempt for human life.

POUM fighters preparing to go to the front, Barcelona, January 1937. Orwell's head is visible at the rear of the photo.

"A BRAVE AND GIFTED BOY"

Smillie's death is not a thing I can easily forgive. Here was this brave and gifted boy, who had thrown up his career at Glasgow University in order to come and fight against Fascism, [...] and all they could find to do with him was to fling him into jail and let him die like a neglected animal.

George Orwell, *Homage to Catalonia*

The mist of lies

Orwell returned to England after his escape from what he called the "lunatic asylum" of Spain. He and Eileen set up home in the country village of Wallington where he tried to get his account of the Spanish Civil War published. He had already written to Gollancz, his publisher, saying: "I hope I shall get a chance to write the truth about what I have seen. The stuff appearing in the English papers is largely the most appalling lies."

Back in Spain, while Franco's forces strengthened their hold on the country, Orwell's former comrades were being put on trial by the pro-Stalin forces now controlling the Republic. The charges against them were eventually dropped in court when it was shown that their confessions were either forged or made under threat, but many pro-Soviet newspapers reported, in any case, that the accused had been found guilty.

"It gives one the feeling that our civilization is going down into a sort of mist of lies where it will be impossible ever to find out the truth about anything", Orwell wrote to a friend.

Orwell at his desk during a visit to Morocco in 1938: "Writing a book is a horrible, exhausting struggle, like a long bout of some painful illness", he said.

Soviet soldiers pass through Red Square, Moscow, 1941. It became a tradition under Stalin's rule for Red Square to be used as a showcase for Soviet military strength and discipline.

False confessions

There was no escape for the innocent in the Soviet Union where Stalin's political system had total control over the police, the media, and the courts. Opponents – or victims – of the regime were being rounded up daily in the mid-1930s, and **brutalized** by the secret police. Many of them were forced to admit to crimes they had not committed. Through fear of further torture or threats to their loved ones, they agreed to confess their "crimes" in public before being executed.

THE GREAT PURGES

In the mid-1930s Stalin launched a wholesale purge of sections of his own population who were seen as potential threats to his power. These included critics within the Communist Party, leaders of the 1917 Revolution, army officers, intellectuals, peasant groups, those suspected of having private wealth, or anyone with connections to these groups. A culture of terror spread across the Soviet Union. People informed against others to protect themselves, to advance their own careers, or to settle private scores. In this period, Stalin's secret police, the NKVD, carried out arrests, executions, and assassinations. The exact number of those murdered during the purges will never be known, but is generally accepted to be more than two million.

Moscow Show Trials

During Stalin's purges, three public trials were conducted against former colleagues of Stalin. These were held in the capital city, Moscow, between 1936 and 1938. Defendants "confessed" to being in league with Western powers or with supporters of Trotsky in a conspiracy against the USSR.

These events, which helped to reinforce Stalin's power and to crush all public expressions of disagreement, are known as the "Moscow Show Trials". They are vividly represented in *Animal Farm* in Napoleon's own "show trial" in Chapter Seven of the book.

Leon Trotsky (1879–1940), reads a pamphlet entitled "Behind the Moscow Trial" (1936). Whilst in exile, he was sentenced to death in his absence in the August 1936 trial. He was murdered in Mexico in August 1940.

ANIMALS ON TRIAL

During Napoleon's "show trial" his attack dogs carry out the death sentences. The words "without cause" have been secretly added to the commandment on the barn wall "No animal shall kill any other animal".

The four pigs waited, trembling, with guilt written on every line of their countenances. Napoleon now called on them to confess their crimes. They were the same four pigs who had protested when Napoleon abolished the Sunday meetings [...]

When they had finished their confession, the dogs promptly tore their throats out, and in a terrible voice Napoleon demanded whether any other animal had anything to confess [...] And so the tale of confessions and executions went on, until there was a pile of corpses lying before Napoleon's feet and the air was heavy with the smell of blood.

ORWELL'S INSPIRATION

One particular incident sparked off Orwell's story, Animal Farm. In the preface to the 1947 Ukrainian edition, Orwell wrote:

*"On my return from Spain I thought of exposing the Soviet myth in a story that could be easily understood by almost anyone and which could be easily translated into other languages. However, the actual details of the story did not come to me for some time until one day (I was then living in a small village) I saw a little boy, perhaps ten years old, driving a huge cart-horse along a narrow path, whipping it whenever it tried to turn. It struck me that if only such animals became aware of their strength we should have no power over them, and that men **exploit** animals in much the same way as the rich exploit the **proletariat**."*

It was during his time in the village of Wallington that Orwell (seen here with pets, 1922) came up with the basic outline for Animal Farm. Opposite his simple cottage was a range of barns known as "Manor Farm", and the name of "Wallington" is thinly disguised as "Willingdon" in the novel.

As Orwell worked on the plot for his novel he began to focus on the power of modern propaganda. The politicians of the day were in a position to tell lies about their opponents and to have these lies spread instantly to millions, reinforced each day through the newspapers and radio. This awesome power haunted Orwell for the rest of his life and became a major theme in his writings. It is one of the main issues in *Animal Farm*, in Napoleon's speeches, and in the figure of Squealer, Napoleon's **mouthpiece**.

Looking back at the times he lived through, Orwell later wrote of "a nightmare world in which the Leader, or some other ruling **clique** controls not only the future, but the past. If the leader says of such and such an event, 'It never happened' – well it never happened. If he says that two and two are five – well, two and two are five. This prospect frightens me more than bombs."

Europe in flames

As the 1930s ended, Europe faced war across its territories. The Spanish fascists completed their victory in the spring of 1939. Hitler's forces had already **annexed** Austria and invaded Czechoslovakia in 1938. Faced with public outcry against German aggression, the British Prime Minister, Neville Chamberlain, announced that Britain would protect Poland if it, too, was attacked by Germany.

German bombers seek out targets over London during the Battle of Britain, fought from 10 July to 31 October 1940.

In August 1939, Hitler and Stalin signed an agreement not to invade each other's countries. On 1 September, the Nazis marched into Poland. Britain declared war on Germany two days later, on 3 September 1939.

Within months Denmark, Luxembourg, Belgium, the Netherlands, and France fell to the Nazi advance. Germany invaded Norway early in 1940, and British troops were forced to retreat to their own shores from the French coast at Dunkirk in order to prevent a massacre.

ORWELL'S WAR

The Orwells were based in London for most of World War II. George was rejected by the armed services on health grounds. He had been weakened by bouts of bronchitis and pneumonia. Also at this time, doctors found signs of tuberculosis – the disease that eventually killed him.

In the end he joined the local defence forces (the Home Guard) in north London. His experience in Spain earned him the rank of Sergeant, and he threw his energies into organizing the civilian militia. "I can put up with bombs on the mantelpiece", Eileen said, "but I will not have a machine gun under the bed."

Turning the tide

Two events in 1941 turned the tide of the war against Nazi Germany. The first was in June when, instead of invading Britain, German troops launched a surprise attack on the Soviet Union. Hitler believed his forces were now strong enough to fight on all fronts – even against his former ally. His decision forced Stalin to line up his forces alongside the Western Allies in the fight against the Nazis.

On 7 December 1941, Japan launched an unprovoked attack on the US naval base at Pearl Harbor. Japan had signed a pact with Germany and Italy earlier that year.

More than 2,000 servicemen died at Pearl Harbor and on 8 December, US President Franklin D. Roosevelt declared war on Japan. Three days later, Germany and Italy declared war on the United States. The fight was now truly worldwide.

Ein Volk, ein Reich, ein Führer!

The caption on the poster reads *Ein Volk, ein Reich, ein Führer* (One People, One State, One Leader). German Führer Adolf Hitler believed that it was his destiny to lead Germany to absolute power around the world and to eliminate "impure" elements from the human race, such as Jews, gypsies, and the disabled.

Britain's wartime Prime Minister, Winston Churchill, saw the attack on Pearl Harbor and the US war declaration as one of the most important moments of World War II:

So we had won after all! [...] England would live, Britain would live [...] Hitler's fate was sealed.

Pointing the finger

Orwell was now working for the BBC as a producer of Radio Programmes in its Indian section. He selected stories for transmission and organized discussions, but increasingly he felt that his work was not connected to the great events taking place around him.

As British politicians and newspapers began to speak warmly of "our Soviet allies" and the figure of "Uncle Joe" Stalin became an overnight hero, Orwell raged against the blindness of his fellow countrymen: "We are now more or less pro-Stalin", he observed. "This disgusting murderer is temporarily on our side."

Orwell was troubled by how easily public opinion could be changed through propaganda. This frustration finds its way into the portrayal of the sheep in *Animal Farm*, bleating Napoleon's latest slogan over and over without really knowing what it means.

"In five years' time it may be as dangerous to praise Stalin as it was to attack him two years ago", Orwell wrote. "But I should not regard this as an advance. Nothing is gained by teaching a parrot a new word."

George Orwell and colleagues recording a wartime BBC broadcast for the Far East. From left to right, standing, George Orwell, Nancy Parratt, William Empson, sitting, Venu Chitale, J. M. Tambimuttu, T. S. Eliot, Una Marson, Mulk Raj Anand, Christopher Pemberton.

Telling tales

One of Orwell's last tasks before he resigned from the BBC in 1943 was to prepare a series of stories for broadcast. Among these was a fairy tale, *The Emperor's New Clothes* by Hans Christian Andersen. It shows how people can be fooled into believing lies and how it takes a kind of honest innocence to break the spell. Orwell may have had this in mind when he began writing *Animal Farm*.

When Orwell left the BBC he became literary editor for a left-wing magazine called *Tribune*, and wrote a weekly column, "As I Please". In late 1943, with close assistance from his wife Eileen, he began to write his own "fairy story": *Animal Farm*.

"THE EMPEROR'S NEW CLOTHES"

*Andersen's fairy story tells of an Emperor who buys only the finest clothes. He parades in public and lives for the flattery of his people. No one dares criticize him. One day, the Emperor hands over a fortune to two **swindlers** who persuade him they can make a costume of cloth so fine that it is almost invisible. Foolish people will not be able to see it, they tell him. The Emperor sends his servants to see how the work is progressing. They are afraid of looking stupid, so they report back enthusiastically.*

Finally, the Emperor parades his new "clothes" in public. Crowds fill the streets to admire his outfit: "What a long train it has", "How well it fits", they cry. Then, a small child calls out that the Emperor has no clothes. Word spreads and the crowd begins to repeat the same thing. Their Emperor is standing before them naked and ridiculous. He pretends not to hear them and walks past "with greater dignity".

An illustration of *The Emperor's New Clothes*, by the artist Monro S. Orr, taken from the *World's Fairy Book* (1933).

Fabulous creatures

Animal Farm is written as a type of **fable**. It follows the traditional pattern of telling a moral tale using animals and giving them human personalities. Orwell wanted to write "a story that could be easily understood by almost anyone". By transporting his views on the Russian Revolution into a "fairy tale" he found the perfect **medium** for his message.

Animal Farm can be enjoyed as a straightforward story. At the same time it can be read as a carefully constructed **satire**. On each page the reader can see parallels with the political events of the time. Orwell said that of all his books, *Animal Farm* was "the one that I really sweated over".

Orwell tends to his goat, Muriel, in Wallington, 1939.

After twenty years as a writer Orwell was strongly suspicious of political speeches and newspaper reports. He was convinced that most political writers tried to disguise their meanings rather than to spell them out.

Political language in the modern world, he argued in an essay for *Tribune* magazine, "consists less and less of words chosen for the sake of their meaning, and more and more of phrases tacked together like the sections of a **prefabricated** hen-house".

In his essay, "Politics and the English Language", Orwell drew attention to the robot-like qualities of politicians speaking in public:

"[...] one often has a curious feeling that one is not watching a live human being but some kind of dummy: a feeling which suddenly becomes stronger at moments when the light catches the speaker's spectacles and turns them into blank discs which seem to have no eyes behind them. And this is not altogether fanciful. A speaker who uses that kind of **phraseology** has gone some distance towards turning himself into a machine."

Orwell's views on Stalin and the Soviet Union were clear. He believed, in the words of the British politician, Lord Acton, that: "Power tends to corrupt; absolute power corrupts absolutely."

He was convinced that left-wing campaigners around the world had been fooled into thinking that the Soviet Union was a workers' paradise. In many ways they had fooled themselves. They needed so passionately to believe in the existence of a fairer world that they were unable to accept evidence that proved it was not so.

Orwell knew that his arguments in *Animal Farm* would be unwelcome to many. "If liberty means anything at all, it means the right to tell people what they do not want to hear", he insisted.

The 1954 cover of Orwell's classic story, published by Secker and Warburg.

From the essay "Why I Write", George Orwell, 1946:

In a peaceful age I might have written ornate or merely descriptive books, and might have remained almost unaware of my political loyalties. As it is I have been forced into becoming a sort of pamphleteer.

Heroes and Villains

The story of *Animal Farm* moves from **idealism** towards **disillusionment** and tragedy. There will be no fairy-tale ending here. But throughout the story, the majority of the animals remains innocent and generous. While Napoleon, Squealer, and their attack dogs become increasingly sinister and vicious in words and actions, the other creatures continue to throw their hearts into the dream of Animal Farm.

WORKING FOR THE REVOLUTION

The animals refuse to see that they have been betrayed by their leaders and continue to throw their efforts into the dream of a future society:

All that year the animals worked like slaves. But they were happy in their work; they grudged no effort or sacrifice, well aware that everything that they did was for the benefit of themselves and those of their kind who would come after them, and not for a pack of idle, thieving human beings.

Throughout the spring and summer they worked a sixty-hour week [...] This work was strictly voluntary, but any animal who absented himself from it would have his rations reduced by half.

Joseph Stalin (top left) and his Party faithful wave to the crowds in Red Square, Moscow, during a military parade, 1 May 1937.

The **pathos** of the book lies in this contrast between the cynical leadership and the basic good-heartedness of the majority. Orwell never lost his belief in what he called "decent, ordinary people". The trick, he felt, was to prevent these people from being taken in by the promises of power-hungry politicians. In this sense his book is written as a warning for future generations.

As he explained: "I meant the moral to be that revolutions only effect [lead to] a radical improvement when the masses are alert and know how to chuck out their leaders as soon as the latter have done their job."

"I will work harder"

The two carthorses, Boxer and Clover, are at the emotional heart of Orwell's story. Boxer, in particular, lives and dies by his belief that endless self-sacrifice and optimism will ensure the success of Animal Farm. When he finally collapses, he is driven away to the knacker's yard where his corpse will be boiled down for glue. The sound of Boxer's hooves beating against the sides of the van is a final drum roll for the failure of the revolution.

TIME
The Weekly Newsmagazine

The Model Worker

Boxer's heroic work suggests a parallel with the figure of Aleksei Grigorievich Stakhanov, a Soviet miner from the small town of Kadievka. On 31 August 1935, he mined 102 tons (92.5 tonnes) of coal during one shift – 14 times his quota, and a new record for coal production. A month later he beat his own record by a further 50 percent. Stakhanov was celebrated in the press as a "Model Soviet Worker" and his example was used to encourage the population to work harder. Here, he appears on the front cover of the US magazine Time in December 1935.

Two faces of tyranny

There is no shortage of violence in *Animal Farm*. Napoleon's attack dogs with their "menacing growls" and "snapping jaws" prowl across the book's pages. But an equally disturbing threat comes through the manipulation of language itself.

Squealer, Napoleon's mouthpiece, can "turn black into white". His speeches, at decisive moments in the story, calm the animals down and persuade them to believe what they know to be untrue.

In Chapter Three of *Animal Farm*, the pigs take the milk and apples for themselves. The other animals question their behaviour for the first time, and Squealer is sent out to make "the necessary explanation":

> *'Comrades!' he cried. 'You do not imagine, I hope, that we pigs are doing this in a spirit of selfishness and privilege? Many of us actually dislike milk and apples. I dislike them myself. Our sole object in taking these things is to preserve our health [...] Day and night we are watching over your welfare. It is for your sake that we drink the milk and eat those apples.'*

Squealer plays on the animals' trust and their desire to believe – and hope for – the best. He talks to them as if they are children. He makes it appear, at every stage, that their growing unease and moral confusion are the result of their own simplicity. His language always contains an underlying menace or threat: " 'Do you know what would happen if we pigs failed in our duty?' he asks. 'Jones would come back! Yes, Jones would come back!' "

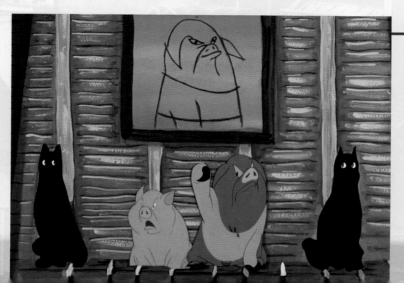

Napoleon and Squealer give a speech from the podium, after the animals take over the farm, from the 1954 cartoon version of *Animal Farm*.

If the threat of Jones is not enough, then, as Orwell explains at the end of Chapter Five, there is always the threat of violence:

"Squealer spoke so persuasively, and the three dogs who happened to be with him growled so threateningly, that they accepted his explanation without further question."

Nazi Propaganda Minister Joseph Goebbels stands at a podium, addressing a rally after Germany and Austria were united in March 1938.

PROPAGANDA

Propaganda is the use of language and images to advance a particular point of view. In itself it is neither good nor bad, but the ruthless use of propaganda by both sides in World War II and during the Cold War (see page 42) has given the word a negative slant.

*Joseph Goebbels, Minister for Public Enlightenment and Propaganda, was a key member of Hitler's regime. Nazi propaganda showed German Jews as sinister, money-grabbing figures who were more like monsters than human beings. The spread of **anti-Semitic** propaganda prepared the German people to participate in the "Final Solution". This was the attempt to exterminate Europe's Jewish population in **concentration camps.** More than six million people were killed.*

Voice in the wilderness

Orwell finished the manuscript of *Animal Farm* in the spring of 1943, but it took two years to get his book into print. Paper was in short supply during the war, and this was one reason for the delay. But the main issue was political. Publishers were reluctant to put out a fiercely anti-Stalin satire at a time when Britain, the United States, and the Soviet Union were united in the fight against Nazism.

Orwell had expected problems. Shortly after completing the manuscript, he wrote to warn off his main publisher, Victor Gollancz, from the project, explaining that *Animal Farm* would be "completely unacceptable politically from your point of view". Gollancz insisted on seeing the novel, but after reading it he wrote straight back saying: "You were right and I was wrong. I am so sorry."

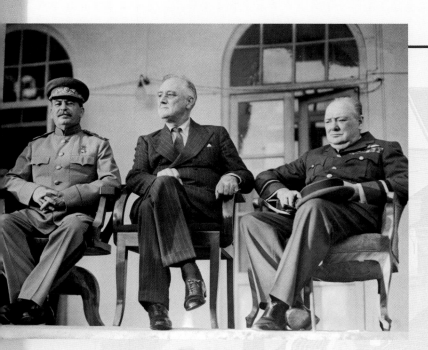

Wartime allies: (from left to right) Premier Joseph Stalin, US President Franklin D. Roosevelt, and UK Prime Minister Winston Churchill meet at the Yalta Conference in the Ukraine, 1945. The meeting marked the high point of Allied unity.

Jonathan Cape publishers looked set to take on *Animal Farm* but because of its sensitive subject matter they asked the advice of "an important official" at the British Ministry of Information. He warned them strongly against publication, saying that Orwell's book was too anti-Soviet, and that representing its leaders as pigs would offend the Soviet leadership!

Some years later, the ministry official who advised Cape, Peter Smollett, was exposed as a Soviet spy working inside the British government. Orwell's fears of political conspiracy were not imaginary.

At one point, Orwell began making plans to print the story himself as a pamphlet, and he arranged to borrow £200 (US$353) to cover the costs. He was determined to publish *Animal Farm* for the very reason that others were determined not to: "I particularly want this book published on political grounds" he explained to his agent.

In the end, Frederick Warburg, who had published Orwell's account of the Spanish Civil War, *Homage to Catalonia*, stepped in. But *Animal Farm* was still not released in Britain until the end of World War II, on August 17, 1945. It was published in the United States a year later. It was the book that finally announced George Orwell to the world.

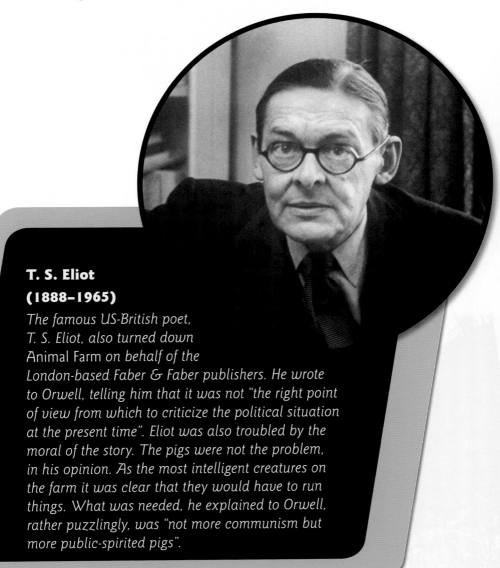

T. S. Eliot

(1888–1965)

The famous US-British poet, T. S. Eliot, also turned down Animal Farm *on behalf of the London-based Faber & Faber publishers. He wrote to Orwell, telling him that it was not "the right point of view from which to criticize the political situation at the present time". Eliot was also troubled by the moral of the story. The pigs were not the problem, in his opinion. As the most intelligent creatures on the farm it was clear that they would have to run things. What was needed, he explained to Orwell, rather puzzlingly, was "not more communism but more public-spirited pigs".*

Orwell did not become an "overnight success" with *Animal Farm*. He had already been struggling as a writer for more than twenty years when the book was finally published in 1945. But his fable touched a nerve and it became an instant classic.

Secker & Warburg printed a first run of 4,500 copies, but early enthusiasm for the book persuaded them to rush out another 10,000 copies. In the United States, a hardback edition of 50,000 launched the book in August 1946. It was then published in a Book of the Month edition with a run of 430,000 paperback copies. *Animal Farm* featured second on the US best-seller list that year, and a writer who had spent his working life away from public attention now found himself at its centre.

An article in *Vogue* magazine described Orwell as "a defender of freedom, even though most of the time he violently disagrees with the people beside whom he is fighting". Another review praised Orwell for his "clever hostility" towards the Soviet Union. Although there was widespread confusion over its message, *Animal Farm* was clearly an important book to read.

Orwell with his adopted son, Richard, in 1946.

COMIC TIMING

After struggling so hard to get the book printed, Orwell was surprised by its reception. "The comic thing", he wrote, "is that after all this fuss the book got almost no hostile reaction when it came out. The fact is that people are fed up with this Russian nonsense and it's just a question of who is first to say: 'The Emperor has no clothes'."

Darkness falls

Orwell was unable to share his success with his wife Eileen who had been his chief critic and supporter in the writing of *Animal Farm*. She died unexpectedly in March 1945 during an operation. The couple had recently adopted a young child, Richard, and Orwell was now left as a single parent, a sad figure whose own health was beginning to fail.

In 1946, he took up a friend's offer and moved to a remote cottage on the Scottish island of Jura. He travelled there with his son, Richard, and a housekeeper. He spent much of his remaining time away from the world, continuing to write articles and reviews, and working on his final novel *Nineteen Eighty-Four*.

Orwell stayed at this house on Jura, Scotland, and wrote *Nineteen Eighty-Four* here between mid-1946 to 1948.

In "Some Thoughts on the Common Toad", an article for *Tribune* in 1946, Orwell wrote:

The atom bombs are piling up in the factories, the police are prowling through the cities, the lies are streaming from the loudspeakers, but the earth is still going round the sun, and neither the dictators nor the bureaucrats, deeply as they disapprove of the process, are able to prevent it.

The Cold War

With the end of World War II, Western hostility shifted away from Germany and Japan, and back towards Russia and the threat of communism. The "Cold War" (a phrase first used by Orwell) began. It was a period of international tension that fell just short of military conflict.

The world had entered the age of the atomic bomb when the United States destroyed the Japanese cities Hiroshima and Nagasaki in 1945. Following this, the United States and Russia began a nuclear **arms race**. Each tried to develop superior weapons and threaten the other into submission.

The nuclear stand-off between East and West, known as the Cold War, lasted for more than forty years with both sides living just minutes from destruction. In the 1980s, the Soviet leader Mikhail Gorbachev tried to reform the Soviet political system but popular unrest led to his overthrow. The Soviet Union finally crumbled in 1990 and the Cold War came to an end.

The devastation of Hiroshima and Nagasaki by atomic bombs in 1945 changed the nature of warfare forever.

THE IRON CURTAIN

In 1946, Britain's wartime leader, Winston Churchill, told a US audience: "An 'iron curtain' has descended across the continent of Europe." The countries of central and Eastern Europe were now under Stalin's control, he explained, and Europe was split down the middle.

In 1949, the United States, Britain, and other West European countries formed NATO (the North Atlantic Treaty Organization) to oppose Soviet influence. The Soviets responded in 1955 with the Warsaw Pact, signed by Albania, Bulgaria, Czechoslovakia, East Germany, Hungary, Poland, Romania, and the Soviet Union.

The wrong message

In this new political climate, *Animal Farm* was misunderstood by many people as an attack on all left-wing attempts to change the world. "Revolutions always fail" was seen as the book's gloomy message. Orwell now found himself associated with views that he had spent a lifetime opposing.

In a letter to the US critic Dwight MacDonald, Orwell explained that things would have turned out differently in his story if the other animals had gathered together at the beginning to oppose the pigs when they stole the apples from them. The problem, he argued, lay in handing over power to a new set of masters: "What I was trying to say was, 'You can't have a revolution unless you make it for yourself.'" Few people listened to him, and *Animal Farm* has most often been read and taught over the past sixty years as a warning against the dangers of political idealism.

East German police repair the Berlin Wall after it was damaged by a young man trying to escape to the West in an armoured car. The Wall divided the city of Berlin in half and was a powerful symbol of the Cold War.

In a preface written in 1947 for the Ukrainian translation of *Animal Farm*, Orwell tried again to set the record straight:

[...] in my opinion, nothing has contributed so much to the corruption of the original idea of Socialism as the belief that Russia is a Socialist country and that every act of its rulers must be excused, if not imitated. And so for the past ten years I have been convinced that the destruction of the Soviet myth was essential if we wanted a revival of the Socialist movement.

The worst of all possible worlds

Despite his attempts to keep hope alive, Orwell's own visions were falling into deep **pessimism**. His final book, *Nineteen Eighty-Four*, is a **dystopian** account of a future world, now divided into three main power blocs, all constantly on the verge of war.

Spies, visual surveillance, and the "thought police" monitor the population. The main character, Winston Smith, works for the Ministry of Truth, or Minitrue. On the vast white concrete walls of the ministry three slogans are inscribed:

WAR IS PEACE.
FREEDOM IS SLAVERY.
IGNORANCE IS STRENGTH.

"If you want a picture of the future", an official tells Winston, "imagine a boot stamping on a human face – for ever".

One of Orwell's most famous slogans is "Big Brother is watching you", seen here in the film version of *Nineteen Eighty-Four*.

Nineteen Eighty-Four describes a world where people can no longer tell the difference between truth and lies. They cannot trust their own ideas, and they have lost the ability even to explain to themselves why this is happening. Orwell called this process "Doublethink" (see page 45).

In the United States, *Nineteen Eighty-Four* became one of the most widely-read novels of all time. By 1970 it had sold more than 8 million copies, and in 1984 the book rose to the top of the best-seller lists.

DOUBLETHINK

Orwell describes "Doublethink" in Chapter Three of *Nineteen Eighty-Four*:

> *To know and not to know, to be conscious of complete truthfulness while telling carefully constructed lies, to hold simultaneously two opinions which cancelled out, knowing them to be contradictory and believing in both of them, to use logic against logic [...] Even to understand the word 'doublethink' involved the use of doublethink.*

Lost books

Seven months after *Nineteen-Eighty Four* was published, Orwell was taken into a London hospital suffering from severe tuberculosis. His health had been in decline for many years, but he refused to accept the inevitable. He told friends that he did not believe a man could die when he had a book inside him – and he had five! He even chose to marry again, to Sonia Brownell, in a bedside ceremony at University College Hospital, at the end of 1949.

Despite his fiery spirit, Orwell died in London on 21 January 1950, at the age of 46.

Sonia Brownell married Orwell just weeks before his death in 1950.

Happy endings on the farm

Orwell's vision of the future involved a world where truth was turned on its head. He might not have been surprised, then, to see what became of *Animal Farm*, his personal favourite amongst his novels.

After World War II, the British government funded a political cartoon strip based on *Animal Farm*. They used it as anti-communist propaganda across Asia, Africa, and South America.

In England, a team that wanted to buy the screen rights to *Animal Farm* approached Orwell's widow, Sonia. She did not know that they worked for the United States' Central Intelligence Agency (CIA), and were carrying out instructions from Howard Hunt at the CIA's Psychological Warfare Workshop. He planned to use *Animal Farm* as propaganda against the spread of communism. Hunt worked behind the scenes in US intelligence for more than three decades before being jailed for his role in the 1972 **Watergate** break-in, which led to the downfall of President Richard Nixon.

Senator Joseph McCarthy, seen here chairing the House Un-American Activities Committee, 1950. He became a powerful figurehead in the hunt for US communists and their friends during this period.

WITCH-HUNTS

*In 1950, US Senator Joseph McCarthy launched a public enquiry to root out communists and their sympathizers, known as the House Un-American Activities Committee. This turned into a "**witch-hunt**". The enquiry damaged many people's reputations, and some were pressured to condemn their own friends.*

In an atmosphere of public hysteria, the socialist writer Arthur Miller wrote a play called The Crucible. It is based on the Salem witch trials of 1692 in which people were tortured and killed for alleged association with witches. Despite its disguised setting, the play's message and its link to the McCarthy witch-hunts was clear.

The CIA-funded cartoon version of *Animal Farm* appeared in 1954 with the ending changed. Instead of Orwell's grim conclusion that pigs and humans – communists and capitalists – have become pretty much the same, the cartoon has a happy ending with the pigs overthrown and freedom triumphing. Asked why he had changed the conclusion, co-director John Halas explained: "You cannot send home millions in the audience being puzzled."

A paperback edition of Orwell's work, published in 1956 at the height of the Cold War, includes his famous claim that "every line I have written since 1936 has been written, directly or indirectly, against **totalitarianism**", but it deletes the rest of the sentence: "*and for democratic socialism as I understand it*".

The playwright and author of *The Crucible*, Arthur Miller, faces the House Un-American Activities Committee in 1956. He was found guilty of supporting communist ideas, but the verdict was overturned a year later.

BIG BROTHER IS WATCHING YOU

*J. Edgar Hoover, the head of the **Federal Bureau of Investigation (FBI)**, ordered a file to be kept on Orwell and his writings. Intelligence agents infiltrated George Orwell societies at US campuses during the 1960s and 1970s in case they were being used as secret socialist meeting places.*

The most recent cartoon version of *Animal Farm*, broadcast in 1999, ends with a "perfect family" – Mum, Dad, and the kids – driving up through the farm gates in an open-topped car to take charge of the animals.

These attempts to change the meaning of Orwell's writings merely emphasize the importance of his message.

The pen and the sword

George Orwell was a difficult man, to friends and enemies alike. He was full of opinions, angry, and uncompromising. His friend from childhood, Cyril Connolly, once said that Orwell "would not blow his nose without moralising on conditions in the handkerchief industry". The writer, V. S. Pritchett, said of Orwell that "he dislikes his own side more than the enemy".

Since his death there has been a tendency to emphasize Orwell's strengths and to hide his weaknesses, to the point where he has often been referred to in school textbooks as a "saint". A book on his reputation as a writer, published in 1989, refers to him in its title as "St George".

Orwell began one of his final essays, on the Indian political leader Mahatma Gandhi, with the words: "Saints should always be judged guilty until proved innocent." It may be best to look at Orwell the man in a similar way. He would not have enjoyed our exaggerated flattery. He would have suspected our motives and wondered what we were up to.

Orwell at work in 1945. In his 1946 essay "Why I Write", Orwell said he wanted to "alter other people's ideas of the kind of society they should strive after".

ORWELL'S LIST

In 1991, documents were found showing that after the end of World War II Orwell had passed on to a government ministry a list of people he thought were "communist sympathizers". Some people see this as a shameful action from a man who condemned spies and informers in his own writings. Others believed that Orwell's concerns over Soviet spying in post-war Britain justified his action.

Sixty years after his death, writers are still encouraged to look at Orwell's work for a model of how to write clearly and honestly. His essay "Politics and the English Language" is still recommended to would-be journalists. "Political language", he argued, "is designed to make lies sound truthful and murder respectable, and to give an appearance of solidity to pure wind. One cannot change this all in a moment, but one can at least change one's own habits."

The Cold War is over, and 1984 passed by more than twenty years ago, but Orwell's writings still speak to us openly and clearly about our hopes for a better future and the risks we face in trying to make it happen.

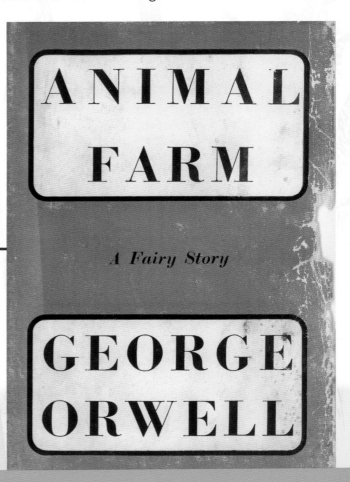

ANIMAL FARM

A Fairy Story

GEORGE ORWELL

The first edition of Orwell's masterpiece, published in 1945 by Secker and Warburg. The Queen was one of its early readers.

In his essay "Why I Write" Orwell said:

My starting point is always a feeling of partisanship, a sense of injustice. When I sit down to write a book, I do not say to myself, 'I am going to produce a work of art'. I write it because there is some lie that I want to expose, some fact to which I want to draw attention, and my initial concern is to get a hearing.

TIMELINE

1903	Eric Arthur Blair is born 25 June in Motihari, India. Mother, Ida Blair, returns to England to bring up children.
1914	World War I begins.
1917	Russian Revolution, February and October.
1917–1921	Attends Eton College as a Kings Scholar.
1921	Joins Indian Imperial Police in Burma and serves as Assistant Superintendent until his resignation in 1927.
1922	Stalin becomes leader of Soviet Communist Party.
1928–1929	Lives in Paris and London, works in low-paid jobs. Begins writing articles and reviews.
1933	Hitler becomes Chancellor of Germany, 1 January.
1933	*Down and Out in Paris and London* published by Victor Gollancz, January. Eric Blair chooses pen name George Orwell.
1934	*Burmese Days* is published in United States by Harper Brothers, October.
1935	Two novels are published in Britain, *A Clergyman's Daughter* and *Burmese Days*. Orwell works in London bookshop, part-time writing, and tramping.
1936	New novel, *Keep the Aspidistra Flying*, is published in April. Marries Eileen O'Shaughnessy, 9 June, and moves to Wallington. Leaves for Spain in December to cover Civil War as journalist. Enlists on the side of the Republic with POUM militia.
1936	Spanish Civil War begins, July.
1937	Orwell begins to plan story based on animals after seeing a boy whip his carthorses in Wallington.
1937	*The Road to Wigan Pier* is published in March. Shot in throat by sniper while fighting on Aragon front, 20 May. Returns to England in June.
1937	German airforce bomb Guernica, Spain, April.
1938	*Homage to Catalonia* is published by Fredric Warburg, April. Tuberculosis (TB) is diagnosed, lengthy treatment at sanatorium. Convalescence in Morocco, September to March 1939.
1939	*Coming Up for Air* is published in June. Orwell refused for National Service on health grounds.

KEY	World history
	Local/national history (Russia/SovietUnion)
	Author's life
	Animal Farm

1939	End of Spanish Civil War. General Franco establishes military dictatorship. Hitler and Stalin sign non-agression pact. Outbreak of World War II.
1940	Moves to London and joins civilian defence forces (Home Guard). Book of essays, *Inside the Whale*, is published in March.
1940	Battle of Britain, June–October.
1941	Joins British Broadcasting Corporation (BBC). Publishes essays on socialism and English nation, *The Lion and the Unicorn*.
1943	Resigns from the BBC.
1943	Begins writing *Animal Farm* and works as Literary Editor for left-wing periodical, *Tribune*.
1944	Orwells adopt son, Richard Horatio Blair.
1944	Completes manuscript of *Animal Farm* and begins lengthy search for publisher.
1945	Eileen dies during operation, 29 March.
1945	Germany surrenders, 7 May.
1945	*Animal Farm* published in the United Kingdom, in May, and receives widespread acclaim.
1946	Retreats to Scottish island, Jura, with son Richard. Begins work on "novel about the future".
1946	*Animal Farm* is published in United States in August. Chosen as Book of the Month and ranks as second best-seller in United States for the year.
1947	Completes draft of *Nineteen Eighty-Four*. Treated for TB of the left lung, Hairmyres Hospital, Glasgow.
1949	*Nineteen Eighty-Four* is published in June in the United Kingdom and United States. It is an instant best-seller. Orwell receives treatment for TB. Marries Sonia Brownell, 13 October, in bedside ceremony.
1950	Dies of pulmonary tuberculosis, London, 21 January. Buried in Sutton Courtenay, Berkshire.
1954	Cartoon version of *Animal Farm* is screened.
1956	Stalinism is denounced at Soviet Communist Party Congress.

The edition used in the writing of this book was published in London, by Penguin, 1987.

Other works by George Orwell

Down and Out in Paris and London (Gollancz, 1933)
A Clergyman's Daughter (Gollancz, 1935)
Burmese Days (Gollancz, 1935)
The Road to Wigan Pier (Gollancz, 1937)
Homage to Catalonia (Secker and Warburg, 1938)
Coming Up for Air (Secker and Warburg, 1939)
Inside the Whale and Other Essays (Gollancz, 1940)
Why I Write (Gangrel, 1946)
Nineteen Eighty-Four (Secker and Warburg, 1949)
Complete Works of George Orwell (Secker and Warburg, 1998)

Books about Orwell and *Animal Farm*

Teenage readers

Middleton, Haydn. *Creative Lives: George Orwell*. (Heinemann Library, 2002)

Gross, Miriam, ed. *The World of George Orwell*. (Weidenfeld & Nicholson, 1971)

Adult readers

Bloom, Harold, ed. *George Orwell's Animal Farm: Modern Critical Interpretations*. (Chelsea House, 1999)

Bowker, Gordon. *George Orwell*, (Abacus, 2003)

Crick, Bernard. *George Orwell: A Life*. (Secker & Warburg, 1980)

Meyers, Jeffrey, ed. *A Reader's Guide to George Orwell*. (Thames & Hudson, 1975)

Taylor, D. J. *Orwell: The Life*. (Chatto & Windus, 2003)

Orwell websites

George Orwell Archive: http://orwell.ru
  This is a comprehensive website, which includes a complete library of Orwell's work including novels, essays, articles, poems, and reviews.

George Orwell: http://www.k-1.com/Orwell
  Includes a great links section, essays on Orwell's influences, and a discussion board.

Spark notes on Animal Farm: http://www.sparknotes.com
  Excellent online study guide, which includes a plot overview, analysis of the major characters and themes, and a section explaining important quotations.

Movies

1984 (1954)
  Directed by Rudolph Cartier and starring Peter Cushing.

Animal Farm (1954)
  An animated adaptation of Orwell's famous novel (see page 47).

Nineteen Eighty-Four (1984)
  Directed by Michael Radford and starring John Hurt, this is a powerful adaptation.

Animal Farm (1999)
  The latest adaptation of this novel, starring an array of famous actors including Kelsey Grammer as Snowball and Patrick Stewart as Napoleon.

Allies relating to Great Britain and its allies in World War I and II

ally friend, fighting on the same side

analysis interpret or explain something

annex control, or take possession of territory

anti-Semitic having aggression or hatred towards people because they are Jewish

appendicitis inflammation of the appendix

arms race attempt by opposing nations to get hold of superior military equipment

Aryan person of Caucasian race not of Jewish descent

authoritarian forcing power or authority on to people under one's control

Bolshevik member of the Russian Social Democratic Party, which seized power in the Revolution of 1917

British Empire countries across the world ruled by Great Britain from around the early 1700s to the mid-1900s

bronchitis illness affecting the throat that causes coughing and muscle spasm

brutalize treat brutally

capitalism economic and political system based on the right to private ownership and profit

clique small, close-knit group of people

Cold War state of political hostility existing between the Soviet Union and the United States after World War II and only ending in 1990 with the collapse of communism

colonize establish control over a country thereby making it a colony

collective for, or including, everyone

communism economic and political system based on collective ownership with profits shared amongst everyone

comrade fellow socialist or communist

concentration camp camp for imprisoning political prisoners or persecuted minorities, such as the Jews in Nazi Germany

conform follow rules, standards, or laws

coolie hired labourer or carrier of burdens

cult system of religious devotion directed towards a particular figure or object

destitution extremely poor and lacking the basic means to provide for oneself

dictatorship political system in which the ruler or rulers act with total power to impose their wishes upon the people

disillusionment disappointing loss of a belief or an ideal

dystopia imaginary place or society in which everything is bad

elite select, or chosen few, at the top of society

exploit make use of for one's own benefit

fable simple story that carries a moral message or useful lesson

fascism system of government in which the idea of "the nation" is central and the leader rules with absolute authority

Federal Bureau of Investigation (FBI) Federal criminal investigative and intelligence agency, which is the principal investigative arm of the United States Department of Justice (DOJ)

idealism representation of things in an ideal form

ideology system of ideas and beliefs

imperialism system under which a nation or empire forces its rule on to other countries using military power

Left, **left-wing** on the side of radical, reforming, or socialist beliefs

maltreat treat cruelly or with violence

manipulate alter or present something so as to mislead

mannerisms frequent gesture or way of speaking or behaving

medium way of doing something

monarchy system of government in which a king or queen is the ruler or head of state

mouthpiece person who speaks on behalf of another person or organization

Nazism political principles implemented by Adolf Hitler and his followers, asserting Aryan racial superiority, and promoting totalitarianism and the expansion of the German state

pamphleteer writer of pamphlets, especially controversial political ones

paranoia condition of the mind in which people experience illusions of unlimited power or serious threats to their well-being

partisanship have strong support for a party, cause, or person

pathos creating a sense of pity or sadness

patriotic devoted to and vigorously supporting one's country

pen name name used by a writer instead of his or her real name often to hide the writer's identity

pessimism lack of hope or confidence in the future

philosopher someone who thinks deeply about basic ideas concerning the world and human experience

phraseology choice or arrangement of words

prefabricate manufactured sections of a building to enable easy assembly on site

privilege special right, advantage, or benefit

proletariat member of the working-classes

propaganda information, often of a misleading or biased nature, used to promote a political cause or point of view

prose ordinary written or spoken language

public school private fee-paying secondary school. Students can also win a special place, or scholarship, through educational achievements.

purge remove a group of people considered undesirable from an organization or place

racket shameful scheme or lie

regime government, especially an authoritarian one

republic country in which power is held by the elected representatives of the people and not by a supreme ruler

Russian Revolution overthrow of the Russian monarchy in two phases in 1917, which led to the establishing of a new communist nation: the Soviet Union

satire work of art in which foolishness or corrupt behaviour by individuals or groups is exaggerated and reduced to ridiculousness

socialism belief in a social system that aims to benefit the whole population through a fairer distribution of wealth and opportunity

squalor miserable and dirty conditions

Stalinism system of government associated with the rule of Joseph Stalin. Stalinism indicates the absolute rule of the leader, the suppression of opposing viewpoints, the control of all public information, and a permanent state of fear among the population.

strike (of employees) refuse to work as a form of organized protest

surveillance close observation, especially of a suspected spy or criminal

swindler person who commits a fraudulent scheme or action

totalitarian system of government in which absolute control is exercised over the thoughts and actions of the population. "Totalitarianism" is often linked to Stalinism and Nazism.

tramping travelling from place to place on foot, with no permanent home, and usually without money or employment

tsar emperor of Russia before the 1917 Revolution

underclass very poorest members of society, often hidden from the view of "ordinary" people

utopian describing an ideal or perfect world

Wall Street Crash stock-market crash of late October, 1929, when share prices on the New York Stock Exchange (NYSE) collapsed

Watergate political scandal in the United States which led to the resignation of President Richard M. Nixon, on 9 August 1974, and numerous other high profile Government officals

witch-hunt campaign directed against a person or group holding views considered a threat to society

World War I one of the bloodiest wars of all time, from 1914 to 1918, in which more than eight million soldiers died and over twenty million were injured in battle